I0559631

BOOKS, BALL AND BUSINESS

THE TRIPLE THREAT PLAYBOOK
FOR BUILDING WEALTH BEYOND TALENT.

WRITTEN BY:
WANDA RUSSELL AND PRESTON RUSSELL

Books, Ball and Business

The Triple Threat Playbook
for Building Wealth Beyond Talent.

Written By: Wanda Russell and Preston Russell
Edited By: Aaron C. Butler

ISBN: 9781967082469 (Paperback)
ISBN: 9781967082476 (eBook)
Library of Congress Control Number: 2025915079

Printed in the United States of America

My Dual Career
Upper Marlboro, MD 20774

MyDualCareer.com

BookButler Publishing Company
Upper Marlboro, MD 20774

TheBookButler.com

My Dual Career titles may be purchased in bulk for educational,
business, fundraising, or sales promotional use. For information,
please email: info@mydualcareer.com

Dedication

This book is lovingly dedicated to the foundation of our family, our biggest cheerleaders, and our lifelong supporters:

To **Oris, James**, and **Lucille**—my amazing grandparents and my mom's parents. Thank you for the sacrifices, the lessons, the love, and the unwavering belief in every dream we've dared to dream. Your legacy lives in every page of this book.

To my mother's siblings—**Arcelia, Sheron, and Eastmond**—thank you for always being there, cheering us on, and walking this journey with us. Your encouragement has meant more than words can express.

To our extended **family and friends**, and to the **community** that continues to support and uplift us—you are part of this story too. Your faith in us fuels our mission to inspire others.

To my wife, **Caitlin**—thank you for your love, support, and for walking this journey beside our family. Your presence adds so much strength to everything we do.

We also want to acknowledge someone very special—my father. He has been our biggest supporter throughout this journey. As a guidance counselor, he didn't just pour wisdom into me—he poured into generations of students, helping them believe in themselves and make smart decisions for their futures. His encouragement helped shape not only this book, but the foundation it stands on.

And to **Goldey-Beacom College**, where I received the education and foundation that helped support the writing of this book—thank you for helping shape the path that brought us here.

This book is not just ours. It's for all of us.

Table of Contents

Introduction:

The Triple Threat Mindset

This book started with a conversation with my mom.

We've always shared a close bond—not just as family, but as partners in growth. From a young age, my mom poured wisdom into me: teaching me about discipline, education, money, faith, and the mindset it takes to build something that lasts. And over the years, I didn't just listen—I applied it. That guidance helped shape me into the business owner I am today.

So, we decided to write this book together.

Books, Ball and Business is more than just a catchy title—it's the blueprint for how I was raised, and how I now live. This book is our way of passing that mindset on to you. It's part memoir, part manual. I'm sharing the real lessons I've learned—and what I'm still learning—as I build my future, with my mom still guiding and supporting me every step of the way.

Whether you're dribbling a basketball, painting murals, singing on a stage, or crushing your grades, this book is here to show you how education, talent, and entrepreneurship can work together to help you build lasting wealth. This isn't just a motivational speech. It's a playbook.

So, what does it mean to be a *Triple Threat*? It means you're not putting all your dreams in one basket. You're not just banking on going pro, becoming famous, or hoping someone will discover your talent. You're building *multiple paths* to success. Think of it like this:

- **Books** sharpen your mind.

- **Ball** fuels your passion.

- **Business** builds your future.

When you combine all three, you become unstoppable.

The Triple Threat Mindset is about having options, confidence, and control. You're not waiting for opportunities—you're creating them. You're using your education to understand contracts, your talent to get noticed, and your entrepreneurial mindset to turn ideas into income. It's about becoming the CEO of your own life.

Whether you end up on a professional team, launching your own company, or changing the world in your own way, this book will help you stay ready. Because life isn't just about Plan A. It's about being so prepared, you've got Plans B, C, and D lined up and ready to go.

Let's dive into what it really means to live with the Triple Threat Mindset—and how you can start today.

Chapter 1:

Books — Why Education Still Wins

You might hear people say, "School isn't for everybody," or, "You don't need a degree to be successful." While there may be some truth in those statements, one thing remains clear: **education will always give you options**. And in life, options are powerful.

Knowledge Is Your First Investment

Education is the first form of wealth you can start building—and no one can take it away from you. Whether you're learning in a classroom, online, through mentorship, or even trial and error, what you learn becomes your toolbox for the future. It's how you gain confidence, make informed decisions, and recognize opportunity when it comes.

When you're educated, you understand contracts before signing them. You read financial statements. You learn how to manage your time and resources. You think critically, problem-solve creatively, and express yourself clearly. These are all tools that every entrepreneur, artist, athlete, and leader needs.

Education Is Bigger Than School

Let's be clear: *books* don't only mean school textbooks. "Books" represent your willingness to learn—constantly. Maybe you're into real estate, hair styling, gaming, or music production. Learn everything about it. Watch tutorials. Read about people who've done it successfully. Ask questions. Take courses. Education is ongoing, and it's something you build into your lifestyle—not just something you do for a diploma.

School as a Training Ground

Middle school and high school aren't just about getting good grades. They're where you start developing habits and discipline that carry into adulthood. Deadlines, group projects, showing up on time— those aren't just school rules. They're life lessons. And if you're an athlete or artist, school gives you structure, support, and exposure you wouldn't get otherwise.

Also, let's not forget scholarships. Strong grades and leadership can open doors to free money for college. That's less debt and more freedom when you graduate.

Your Brain Is Your Best Asset

Every business mogul, celebrity, or professional athlete has to make decisions. And if you don't have the education to back you up, you risk signing away your money, your brand, or your rights. That's why staying sharp mentally is just as important as staying in shape physically.

There's a reason athletes go back to college. There's a reason CEOs read books constantly. Learning never stops.

Bottom Line: Bet on Your Brain

No matter where life takes you—on the court, in the studio, in the kitchen, or in the boardroom—your education will go with you. It's your *Plan A, B, and C* all wrapped into one. And it doesn't have to look like everyone else's path. What matters is that you stay curious, stay coachable, and stay committed to growth.

Because when you invest in your mind, you're preparing yourself to win—again and again.

Chapter 2:

Ball — Passion, Talent, and the Power of Purpose

"Ball" isn't just about basketball—it's a symbol for your talent, passion, and purpose. Whether your "ball" is painting, cooking, singing, dancing, coding, or athletics, this chapter is about recognizing what makes you come alive and using it as fuel for your future.

Talent Alone Isn't Enough

You may be the most talented person in your class, school, or city—but without discipline, strategy, and vision, talent fades. Plenty of people are born with gifts. The ones who stand out are the ones who do the work. That's where purpose and passion come in.

Passion keeps you going when things get hard. Purpose helps you aim that passion in the right direction.

Your Talent Can Open Doors

Talent is often your first introduction to the world. It gets you noticed. It creates connection. It gives people a reason to listen. But what happens after they're watching?

If you're an athlete, maybe you get recruited. If you're a musician, maybe you land a gig. That's momentum—but momentum needs management. That's where education and business come in. Your "ball" opens the door. What you do next keeps you in the room.

Practice Like a Pro

Treat your talent like it's already your profession. Show up early. Stay late. Study the greats. Work when no one's watching. If you want people to invest in your future, you have to invest in it first.

When you combine your talent with education and business savvy, you're building more than a moment—you're building a brand.

Talent Can Be Monetized

Your gift can become a business. If you're an artist, you can sell your art. If you cook, you can launch a food brand or social media. If you're an athlete, you can offer personal training or create content around your journey.

Turning your talent into income is not about "selling out"—it's about building a future from something you love. That's powerful.

You Don't Have to Be Famous to Be Successful

Not everyone will go pro. Not everyone will become a household name. But that doesn't mean you can't make money, build influence, and do what you love for a living. You can build your own lane.

And the best way to secure your lane is to combine your gift (*ball*) with your knowledge (*books*) and your hustle (*business*).

Chapter 3:

Business — Why a Business Makes You a Triple Threat

A triple threat isn't just about being talented in multiple areas. It's about being strategic. Having a business doesn't mean you give up your dream—it means you build a foundation that can support it. Your business is your backup plan, your bridge, and your launchpad all in one.

Business Is Control

When you own a business, you control your schedule, your income, and your direction. That doesn't mean it's easy—but it means you're calling the shots. No more waiting on someone to discover you, sign you, or pick you. You pick yourself.

Whether your business is selling custom sneakers, running a tutoring service, making music beats, or starting a clothing brand, it becomes your platform. It teaches you how to manage money, market yourself, and make decisions. These are skills that will serve you for life.

Why a Business Matters—Even If You "Make It"

Let's say you *do* make it big. You land that record deal, sign with a team, or get your art featured on a major platform. Amazing! But what happens when the spotlight dims? What happens when you're no longer trending or when your contract ends?

That's where your business keeps you grounded. You're not starting from scratch—you already have a second stream of income, a loyal audience, or a product line. Your brand becomes bigger than one job or title. You're building legacy, not just fame.

Business Builds Identity

A business helps you tell your story your way. You can merge your passions and personality into something that represents you. Whether it's your name on a product, your voice in a podcast, or your message in a mentorship program, it's yours.

And once people trust your business, they start to trust *you*. That's when real influence happens.

Grit Is the Glue

Starting a business takes effort, and that's where grit comes in. Grit is passion and perseverance over time. It's what keeps you going when things are hard. A triple threat isn't just smart or talented—they're resilient. They know how to show up, figure it out, and keep building.

Grit separates dreamers from doers. When you develop grit, you're preparing yourself for both the highs and the lows. That mindset makes you unstoppable in business and in life.

Start Now, Not Later

You don't have to wait until you're grown to start a business. You don't need a fancy office or a million-dollar idea. You need a passion, a plan, and the willingness to learn. We'll talk more about how to start in later chapters, but know this: the earlier you start, the further you'll go.

Chapter 4:

Wealth Is Built, Not Given

There's a big difference between being rich and being wealthy. Rich can be temporary. Wealth is something you build, protect, and pass on. And here's the truth: **most wealthy people didn't just get lucky—they got educated, stayed disciplined, and made smart moves over time**.

What Wealth Really Means

Wealth isn't just about money—it's about freedom. It's the freedom to wake up and choose how you spend your day. The freedom to walk away from bad deals. The freedom to help your family, invest in your community, and leave a legacy behind.

Wealth is also about ownership. Do you own your brand? Your ideas? Your time? The more you own, the more control you have. That's why understanding business and financial literacy is so important—it teaches you how to turn income into assets.

The Myths That Hold Us Back

Sometimes we grow up thinking wealth is only for other people. We think it's only for celebrities or people born into it. But wealth is not about where you start—it's about what you build. You don't need to be famous to be financially free.

Don't wait for someone to hand you success. You have to take steps—sometimes small, consistent ones—to build it yourself.

Lessons from the Locker Room to the Boardroom

Look at the athletes who had million-dollar contracts but lost it all. Then look at those who turned their earnings into real estate, clothing brands, tech companies, or schools. What's the difference? *Mindset, education, and strategy.*

The same is true for artists who get record deals or chefs who land TV spots, as an example. Some blow the money and lose it all. Others reinvest, build businesses, and grow something that lasts. It's not about how much you make—it's about how you manage and multiply it.

Wealth Is a Team Effort

You don't have to do it alone. Surround yourself with mentors, advisors, and teammates who know what they're doing. Ask questions. Learn about taxes, contracts, investments, and savings. Build a circle that helps you grow, not drain your energy or bank account.

Grit + Growth = Generational Wealth

Being a Triple Threat takes grit. Grit means doing the hard stuff even when it's not glamorous. It means learning, showing up, failing forward, and staying consistent. Add that to growth—through learning, strategy, and smart decision-making—and you've got the formula for generational wealth.

And that's what this is all about—not just shining today, but setting up your future so your kids, family, and community can shine too.

Chapter 5:

When Plan A Doesn't Work Out

L et's be real—sometimes Plan A doesn't go the way we imagined. You train your whole life to go pro, and you don't get drafted. Or maybe you get drafted, play one or two seasons, and then you're cut. The lights dim, the crowds fade, and suddenly, you're faced with a new reality: *What now?*

This Chapter Is for the Dreamers

This chapter is especially for the athletes, artists, and creatives who gave their all to their craft. You were told you had the talent. You believed in the dream. Then the dream changed—or got delayed. That moment can break you, or it can build you. The choice is yours.

We've seen too many athletes go from seven-figure contracts to zero bank balance. We've seen performers go from sold-out shows to silence. What they often lacked wasn't talent—it was a *Plan B*.

Your Talent Is Still Valuable

Just because Plan A didn't work out doesn't mean you failed. It means you need to pivot. The discipline, focus, and resilience you developed through your talent are transferable. You can apply them to business, leadership, and innovation. Your story isn't over—it's evolving.

Your story can become your product, your brand, your business. People pay for authenticity. They pay for experience. Use what you've been through to help others—and get paid doing it.

The Power of Planning Ahead

Having a backup plan isn't doubting yourself—it's protecting your future. That's why *Books, Ball and Business* works: if one leg of the stool breaks, the others still stand. Education gives you insight. Talent gives you passion. Business gives you options.

The best time to build a Plan B is while Plan A is still in motion. Start the business, explore other skills, invest your money wisely. If the original plan shifts, you're not scrambling—you're stepping into something you've already built.

From Breakdown to Breakthrough

There are so many success stories that didn't start until someone's "Plan A" ended. The player who became a coach. The dancer who launched a wellness brand. The singer who built a studio for young talent. Their Plan B became bigger than their original dream.

And here's the truth: if you have grit, vision, and a strategy, you're never truly starting over. You're starting again—with experience.

Chapter 6:

Bonus Chapter — After the Draft

This one is personal. It's for every athlete who dreamed of going pro, heard their name called on draft night, and then—months or years later—found themselves wondering what's next.

The reality is this: **most professional sports careers are short**. Some end before they even truly begin. Injuries, team cuts, performance pressure, or simply not fitting into a team's future plans can leave you sidelined—and financially, emotionally, and mentally drained.

Drafted Doesn't Mean Done

Getting drafted is a dream come true. But it's not the end goal—it's the starting line. And if you're not prepared with education, financial literacy, and a plan for life beyond the game, the fall can be hard.

You've probably heard the statistics: many athletes are broke within a few years of retiring. Not because they didn't earn enough, but because they didn't build enough. They didn't diversify. They didn't plan.

This chapter is your wake-up call—and your encouragement.

When the Lights Go Out

What happens when your jersey is taken back? When the coaches stop calling? When the fame fades and you're no longer "the next big thing"?

You're still YOU. And that means you still have value. Your experience, your discipline, your story—all of that is powerful when used the right way. The key is to pivot.

Start mentoring. Start coaching. Start a training business. Speak at schools. Launch a podcast. Write a book. Sell a product. Educate yourself in business, finance, and branding. That pivot can turn disappointment into destiny.

WNBA, NFL, Broadway, Record Deals — They're All Similar

It's not just athletes. Dancers, singers, chefs, and actors all face the same cycle. You land a role or a deal, and then it ends. If you didn't build something while the spotlight was on, it's harder to start once it's gone.

The WNBA has athletes working side hustles. NFL players get cut after one or two seasons. Broadway actors hustle between shows. Record label artists lose deals after one album. It's not about *if* the season ends—it's about what you *do* next.

Start Your Plan B While Plan A Is Hot

If you're in the game right now, this is your moment. Use the platform. Use the money wisely. Use your influence to grow something. Don't wait for the contract to expire—start planting seeds now.

Because when you have a plan, you don't panic. You pivot. You build. You grow. That's how you become a true triple threat.

Chapter 7:

The Brand Called You

You are your own brand. Whether you're an athlete, an artist, a gamer, or an entrepreneur—you represent something. And whether you realize it or not, people are already forming an impression of who you are based on how you carry yourself online and in person.

Your brand is the vibe people feel when they hear your name. It's your message, your mission, and your energy. It's in your social media, your handshake, your work ethic, and your voice. Building that brand on purpose—and not by accident—is what separates the good from the unforgettable.

Why Your Personal Brand Matters

In today's world, especially in industries driven by visibility—sports, entertainment, entrepreneurship—your brand can make or break opportunities. You might be talented, but if your reputation is messy or unclear, you'll miss out on partnerships, endorsements, and investments.

People don't just buy what you do—they buy into who you are.

A solid personal brand:

- Builds trust and credibility.

- Attracts the right people and opportunities.

- Makes you stand out from the competition.

- Helps you stay focused and aligned with your goals.

Building the Brand Called YOU

Here's how to get intentional about your image:

1. Know who you are and what you stand for.
   Ask: What do I value? What kind of energy do I bring? What do I want people to say about me when I'm not in the room?

2. Audit your digital footprint.
   Google yourself. Scroll through your social media pages. Would you be proud if a coach, employer, or investor saw this? If not, clean it up.

3. Be consistent.
   People trust what they see repeatedly. If you're positive, insightful, and authentic in one space—carry that same energy everywhere.

4. Share your story.
   Let people know where you came from and what you've overcome. Share wins and lessons. Don't be afraid to be vulnerable. Your journey is powerful.

5. Invest in your growth.
   Take courses, read books, learn skills that align with your brand. Stay relevant and sharp.

6. Create value for others.
   Whether it's through helpful content, inspiration, or mentorship—give back. A powerful brand isn't just about "me"—it's about impact.

7. Protect your name.
   If you have a unique brand name, logo, or slogan, consider trademarking it. Own your IP. Don't let someone else profit off your identity.

Brand vs. Image

Your image is how you look. Your brand is how you live.

Don't confuse style with substance. You can have both. Just make sure the energy you're putting out aligns with the person you truly are and want to become.

Chapter 8:

How to Start a Business While Still in School

You don't have to wait until you graduate to start building your future. Some of the most successful entrepreneurs in the world started young—while still in middle school, high school, or college. You have something powerful that most adults wish they had: time. Use it wisely.

Start With What You Know

You don't need a million dollars or a fancy office to start a business. You just need a good idea and a willingness to learn. The best place to start is with what you already know or enjoy.

Ask yourself:

- What am I good at?

- What do people ask me for help with?

- What do I enjoy doing that others might pay for?

Maybe you're good at tutoring classmates, designing logos, editing videos, braiding hair, fixing tech issues, or making beats. These are all skills you can turn into a service-based business right now.

Or maybe you love sneakers, fashion, or gaming. You could start a resale hustle, a clothing brand, or a social media channel/business. Passion + a plan = potential.

Keep It Simple

Your first business doesn't need to be perfect. It needs to be doable.

Here's a basic formula to get started:

1. Find a problem. What's something people around you struggle with?

2. Create a solution. What can you offer that solves it?

3. Test it. Start with a few people and get feedback.

4. Improve it. Tweak your product or service based on what you learn.

5. Promote it. Use social media, word-of-mouth, or school clubs to spread the word.

6. Keep growing. Reinvest your profits, expand your reach, and keep learning.

It's okay to start small. Maybe you make $50 this week, $200 next month, and $1,000 the next semester. That's how growth works.

Use Your School as a Launchpad

School isn't just a place to learn—it can be a business incubator if you use it right:

- Ask teachers or mentors for advice.

- Join business clubs, or entrepreneur competitions.

- Use class projects to work on your business ideas.

- Network with other students who have skills you don't (like a coder, designer, or editor).

The earlier you start, the faster you learn. And school is the best place to learn while the stakes are low and the resources are free.

Legal Stuff (Don't Skip This)

Even if your business is small, it's smart to learn the basics of setting it up the right way. This protects you and makes you look more professional.

Here are a few simple steps you can look into (with the help of a parent or trusted adult):

- Register a name (DBA or LLC, depending on your state).

- Open a business bank account (never mix it with your personal money).

- Learn the basics of taxes and how to track your income.

- Use tools like Canva for design, Shopify for stores, or Cash App/Venmo for payments.

Don't stress if this sounds like a lot. You don't have to figure it all out today. Just take one step at a time.

Learn by Doing

The best way to become a boss? Act like one. That means:

- Setting goals and deadlines.

- Taking notes on what works and what doesn't.

- Asking for help when needed.

- Treating people well—your customers, your teammates, your supporters.

Every business you start—even if it fails—teaches you something. Every mistake is a lesson. Every win builds confidence.

This is about more than making money. It's about building something that belongs to you.

You're not just a kid with a hustle.

Chapter 9:

Choosing the Right Business Structure

Starting a business is exciting—but before you begin selling products or offering services, it's important to understand how your business is set up legally. This structure affects how you pay taxes, how much personal risk you take on, and how others view your business. In other words, it's a key part of protecting your brand and your future.

Think of choosing a business structure like choosing your uniform. You wouldn't walk into a football game wearing flip-flops—you'd suit up properly. The same goes for business. You want to show up prepared, protected, and professional.

Let's break down the most common types of business structures:

1. Sole Proprietorship

This is the simplest structure—and it's how many people start out.

Pros:

- Easy to set up (no formal paperwork in most cases)
- You're in complete control
- All profits go to you

Cons:

- You're personally responsible for any business debts or legal issues
- Harder to get business loans or investors

Best for:

- Freelancers, tutors, artists, or very small businesses just getting started

2. Limited Liability Company (LLC)

An LLC separates your personal finances from your business finances. That means if your business gets sued or goes into debt, your personal assets (like your car or savings) are protected.

Pros:

- Personal liability protection
- More credibility with clients and banks
- Flexible tax options

Cons:

- Slightly more paperwork than a sole proprietorship
- Annual filing fees in most states

Best for:

- Entrepreneurs who are serious about building and protecting their brand long term

3. Partnership

This structure is for when you go into business with one or more people. You share the profits—and the responsibilities.

Pros:

- Shared skills and startup costs
- Can divide roles (e.g., one handles marketing, one handles finances)

Cons:

- If your partner makes a mistake, you're both legally responsible
- Disagreements can damage the business

Best for:

- Trusted friends or family members with complementary strengths

Tip: Always create a written partnership agreement—no matter how close you are.

4. Corporation (C-Corp or S-Corp)

Corporations are the most formal and complex structure. They're usually for large companies with shareholders and boards of directors. Not usually necessary for young entrepreneurs just starting out.

Pros:

- Strong legal protection
- Easier to attract investors

Cons:

- Lots of paperwork
- Higher taxes and legal fees

Best for:

- High-growth startups looking for big funding

How to Choose the Right One

Ask yourself:

- Do I need legal protection for my personal assets?
- Am I planning to grow this business or keep it small?

- Do I have partners or am I doing this alone?
- Am I ready to handle some basic paperwork and fees?

For most youth and first-time business owners, starting as a sole proprietor or forming an LLC is a strong place to begin.

Take Action

Here's how to move forward:

1. Choose your business name
2. Decide on a structure (Sole Prop, LLC, etc.)
3. Check your state's registration requirements
4. Apply for an EIN (Employer Identification Number) at IRS. gov — it's free!
5. Open a business bank account
6. Keep your personal and business finances separate

Remember: the way you structure your business helps determine how strong and secure it becomes. Protect your hustle like it's worth a million dollars—because one day, it might be.

You're a future mogul in training.

Chapter 10:

Getting Business Funding

You've got the idea. You've built the brand. Now comes a big step: funding your business.

Whether you want to buy equipment, launch a product, or scale your operations, chances are you'll need money. And for many young entrepreneurs, getting funding is one of the toughest parts of the journey.

But here's the good news: there's money out there. You just need to know where to look—and how to prepare.

The Challenges of Getting Business Funding

Let's be real—getting funding isn't always easy. Here are a few common roadblocks:

1. Lack of Credit History

Many young entrepreneurs don't have an established credit record. Lenders often want to see that you've borrowed and repaid money responsibly before handing you any.

2. No Business Track Record

If your business is new, you might not have sales, clients, or traction. Lenders and investors want proof that your business idea works before they invest.

3. Weak or No Business Plan

A business idea in your head isn't enough. You need a clear plan that shows what your business does, who it helps, how it makes money, and how you'll use the funds.

4. Not Knowing Where to Look

Grants, competitions, microloans, pitch events, youth programs—there are options, but many young entrepreneurs don't know they exist.

5. Fear of Rejection

Asking for money can be intimidating. But remember: rejection doesn't mean your idea is bad. It just means it might not be the right fit for that funder. Keep going.

What You Should Have Ready Before You Apply

To increase your chances of getting funded, you need to be organized and confident. Here's what funders want to see:

1. A Solid Business Plan

Include:

- An executive summary
- What your business does
- Who your customers are
- Your marketing plan
- Projected costs, income, and profits
- How much funding you need and how you'll use it

2. A Budget

Break down where every dollar will go—equipment, software, inventory, ads, etc.

3. Proof of Demand

This could be:

- Early sales
- Social media engagement
- Pre-orders
- Testimonials

4. Your Story

Why are you starting this business? What makes you the right person to lead it? Funders invest in people as much as ideas.

5. Business Structure & EIN

Have your business registered and get an EIN (Employer Identification Number) from the IRS. It shows you're official.

6. Separate Bank Account

Keep your business money and personal money separate. It's more professional and makes taxes easier.

7. Credit Info

If applying for a loan, they may check your personal credit. Start building your credit now by managing a student card or bill payments wisely.

Where to Look for Funding

Here are some great starting points:

- Local business pitch competitions
- Youth entrepreneurship grants
- Crowdfunding (GoFundMe, Kickstarter, etc.)
- Microloans through banks or organizations like Kiva
- Small business development centers in your area
- Family and friends (with a written agreement)

Tip: Your school might even have a business pitch program or know about local grants.

Be Creative, Be Brave

Even if you don't get funding the first time, keep building. Show funders that you're serious. Keep records. Track your growth. Follow up.

Sometimes the best funding isn't a loan—it's your own profits. Reinvest what you earn. Keep your expenses low. Let your business fund itself as it grows.

Remember, it's not just about getting money—it's about managing it wisely and showing funders that you're a good investment.

You're not begging—you're building.

Chapter 11:

Protect Your Play
— Understanding
Intellectual Property

You've got ideas. Big ones. Game-changing ones. But here's the truth: if you don't protect them, someone else can claim them. And in the business world, protecting your creativity is just as important as creating it.

That's where intellectual property (IP) comes in.

What is IP?

Intellectual property refers to the things you create with your mind—like your brand name, logo, inventions, songs, videos, clothing designs, poems, business concepts, and more. If it came from your brain and has value, it needs protection.

There are four main types of intellectual property every entrepreneur should know:

1. Copyright

Protects original work—music, writing, videos, art, photography, software, and more.

- Example: You write a poem, design a coloring book, or produce a beat—you automatically own the copyright, but registering it makes it enforceable in court.

- Protects against: Someone using your work without permission or claiming it as their own.

2. Trademark

Protects your brand identity—like business names, logos, taglines, and even unique product packaging.

- Example: You create a logo and a brand name for your clothing line. You trademark it so no one else can legally use that name or design.

- Protects against: Others using similar names or logos that confuse your customers.

3. Patent

Protects inventions, processes, or new products.

- Example: You create a new type of athletic training equipment— you'd apply for a patent to make sure no one else can copy or sell it.

- Protects against: Copycats producing or selling your invention without permission.

4. Trade Secrets

Protects confidential business information that gives you an advantage— like formulas, recipes, or internal processes.

- Example: Your unique smoothie recipe or your strategy for getting clients could be considered a trade secret if it's protected and not shared.

Why Does This Matter?

If you're building something—a brand, a product, a business—you need to think like an owner from the start. That means not just building, but protecting what you build. Imagine launching a brand, gaining followers, and then finding out someone else trademarked your name or copied your content.

Real talk: You don't want to get famous just to lose your rights.

How to Start Protecting Your Ideas

1. Keep records of your work—document your process, drafts, launch dates, and who you share it with.

2. Add copyright notices to your content (e.g., © 2025 Your Name).

3. Use nondisclosure agreements (NDAs) when sharing big ideas with potential collaborators.

4. Check that your business name or logo isn't already taken—search the USPTO database (uspto.gov).

5. Register your copyrights and trademarks when you're ready to grow.

6. Treat your brand like it's valuable—because it is.

Young Creators Are Often Targeted

Don't think you're too young or too small to worry about this. If your idea gains attention, someone might try to copy or steal it. That's why it's better to prepare now.

You worked hard to create your brand, your design, your sound. You deserve to keep ownership and profit from it.

Final Thought: You are the CEO of your creativity. Own it. Protect it. Profit from it.

Chapter 12:

Conclusion — Your Legacy Starts Now

If you've made it this far, you already know something big: you're not waiting for life to happen—you're preparing to own it.

This book isn't just about ideas. It is a playbook—a guide written from the heart of a family that's been walking this journey together. My mother and I came together to share lessons that she poured into me from childhood. Lessons about discipline. About faith. About building something for yourself so you don't have to rely on someone else to define your worth.

But this journey wasn't just between us.

My father has been our biggest supporter—encouraging every dream, showing up at every milestone, offering wisdom and care that shaped not only this book but the entire way I see the world. As a guidance counselor, he didn't just invest in me—he invested in every student who crossed his path. He helped kids dream bigger, plan smarter, and keep pushing even when life pushed back. His impact continues to ripple through every page of this book.

We hope you feel that love, that strength, and that vision as you turn this last page.

You are not just a student.

You are not just an athlete.

You are not just an artist or entrepreneur.

You are a legacy builder.

Every chapter you read—on books, ball, and business—was a blueprint to help you think deeper, dream bolder, and move smarter. We want you to use this knowledge to:

- Graduate with more than just a diploma.

- Chase your dreams with a plan and a purpose.

- Launch something that belongs to you.

- Protect your ideas, brand, and future.

- Become a leader in your community.

You are the CEO of your life. And your legacy starts today—not after college, not after you "make it," but now.

So go ahead—draft that business plan, record that first video, apply for that EIN, host that event, design that logo. Do it scared. Do it unsure. Just do it with heart.

Because when you lead with purpose, power, and persistence—when you combine Books, Ball, and Business—there's no limit to what you can become.

This isn't the end.

It's the beginning.

Now go build your legacy.

About the Author

Wanda Russell is a seasoned business professional with many years of experience spanning Residential and Commercial Real Estate, Life Coaching, and Financial Coaching. As an acclaimed, award-winning Realtor® serving the D.C., Maryland, Delaware, and Virginia metropolitan areas, she has earned a reputation for excellence and is a longstanding member of several respected industry associations.

Balancing her real estate career with entrepreneurial ventures, Wanda is the author of *The Dual Career Real Estate Agent* and *Do the Hustle*—two empowering guides for business professionals pursuing multiple streams of income. She is also the inventor of *Home Design in a Bag*.

Wanda's innovation also includes tools and strategies that support productivity and work-life balance. Her talents even extend into the creative world as a writer of commercial music jingles for businesses. Through real estate investing and home flipping along the East Coast, she teaches others how to build wealth and create lasting financial security.

As a motivational speaker and workshop facilitator, Wanda travels extensively to educate audiences on the importance of financial literacy. Despite her many accomplishments, she remains deeply committed to her faith, family, and community—always finding time to give back and inspire others to define success on their own terms and live a life of purpose and achievement.

Wanda Russell

Business Professional | CEO | Coach | Realtor® | Author | Financial Columnist | Motivational Speaker | Wife | Mother

Preston Russell is a proud native of both Washington, D.C., and New York City. A graduate of Largo High School, he went on to earn an associate degree in Business Administration, a bachelor's degree in Finance, and a master's degree in Finance from Goldey-Beacom College.

A devoted husband and father of two, Preston is known not only for his commitment to family but also for being a steadfast source of support to friends, colleagues, and employees alike.

As a serial entrepreneur, Preston has launched multiple restaurants and mobile food truck businesses, always focused on building "backup plans" and multiple income streams to stay ahead in an ever-changing economy. His tireless work ethic and entrepreneurial drive have earned him features in various newspaper articles recognizing him as a rising star in the business world.

Preston has a deep passion for inspiring the next generation. He actively gives back through mentorship and motivational speaking, particularly around youth empowerment and entrepreneurship. His current mission is to speak to young people about launching businesses early in life and embracing the *Books, Ball, and Business* mindset—becoming a triple threat in today's competitive world.